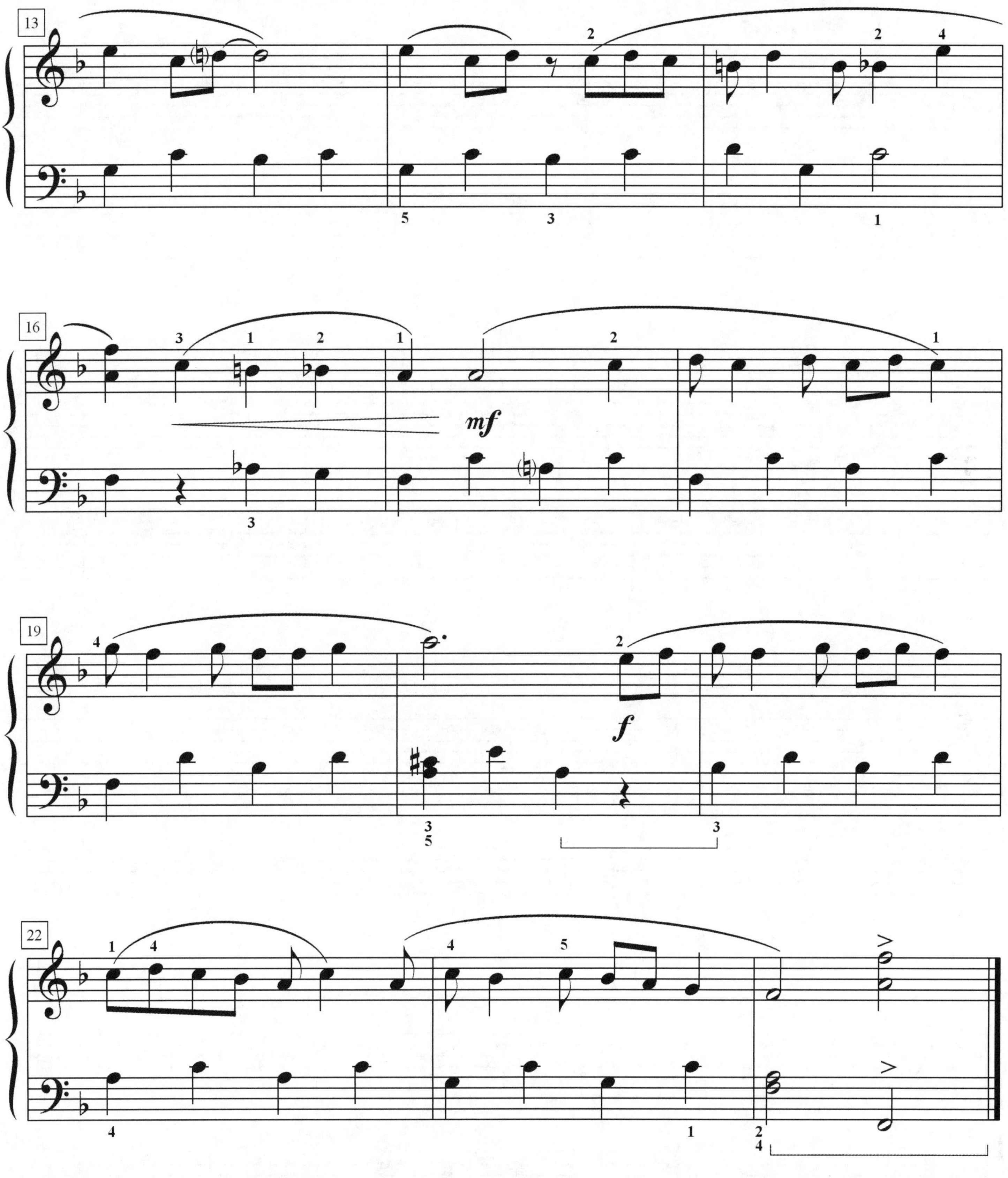

Nappy Lee

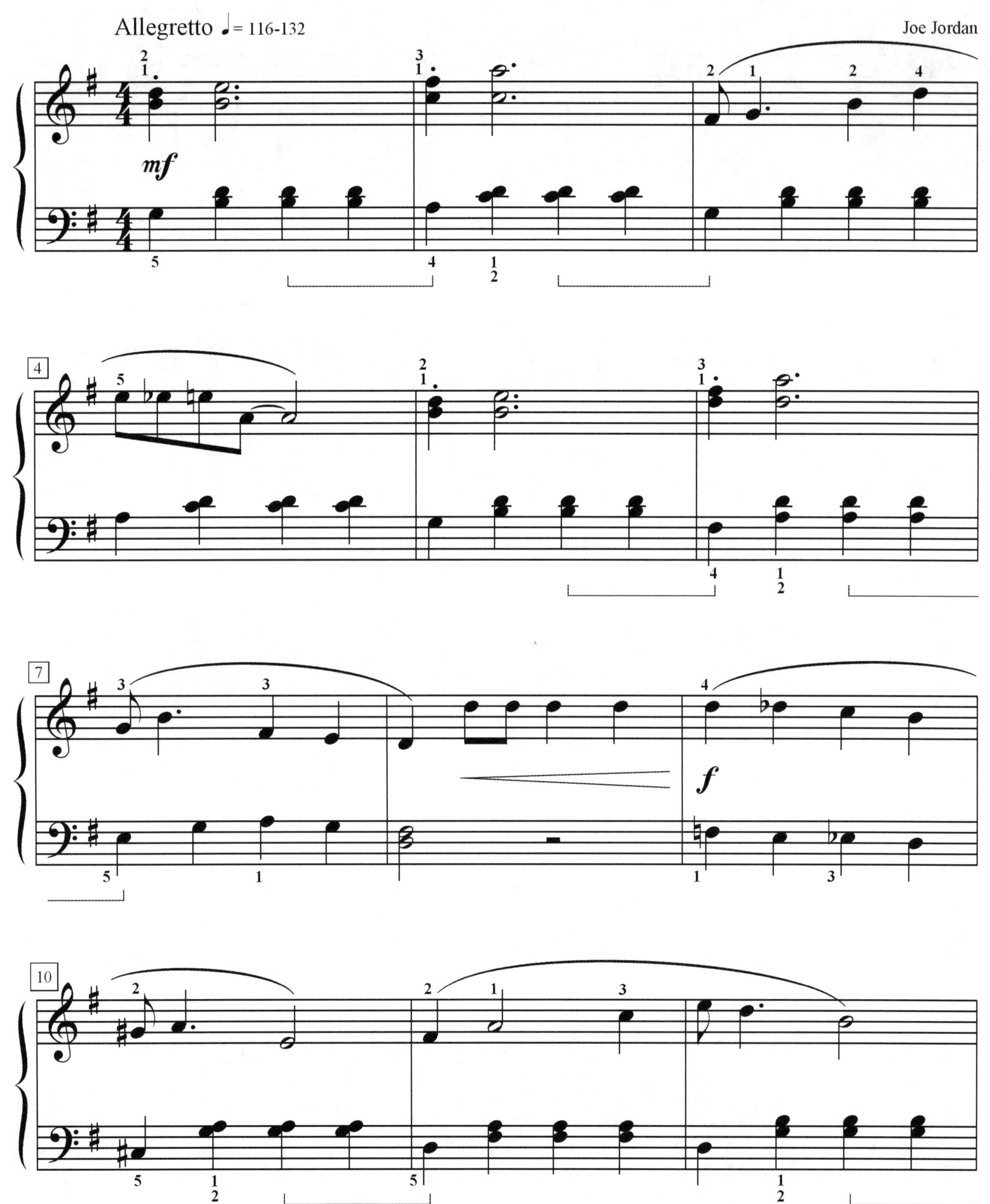

Allegretto ♩ = 116-132
Joe Jordan
mf
f

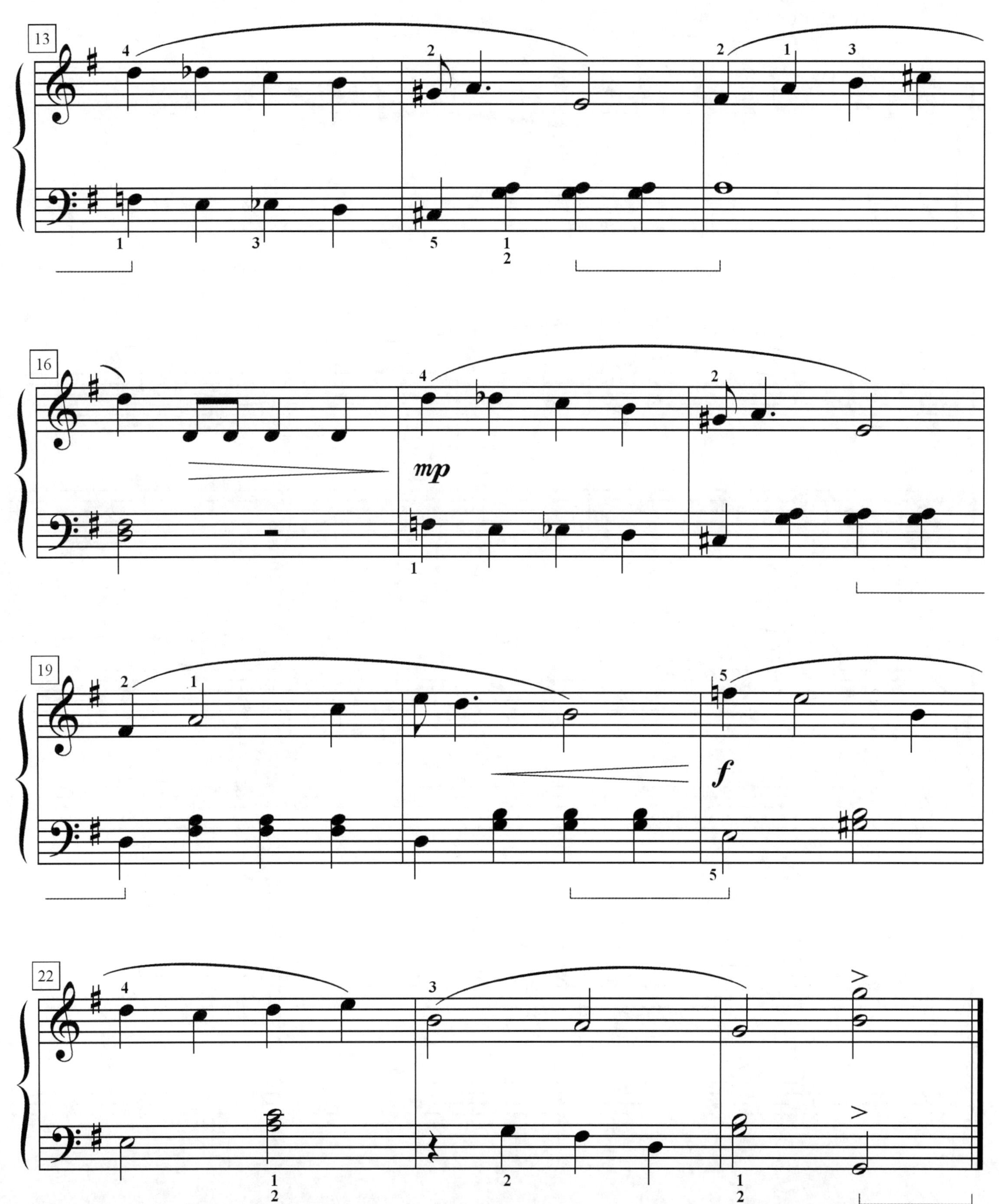

Honeysuckle Rag

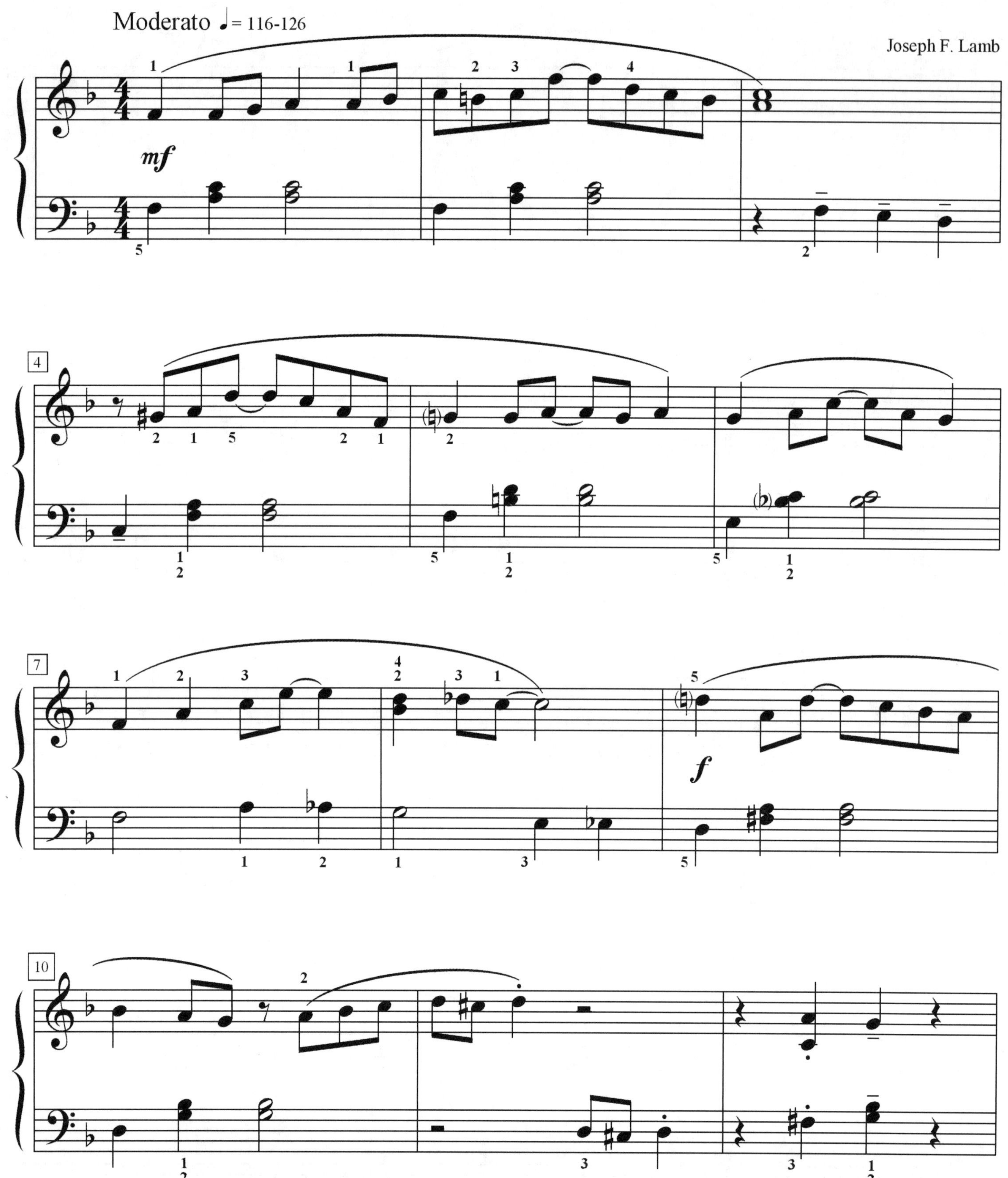

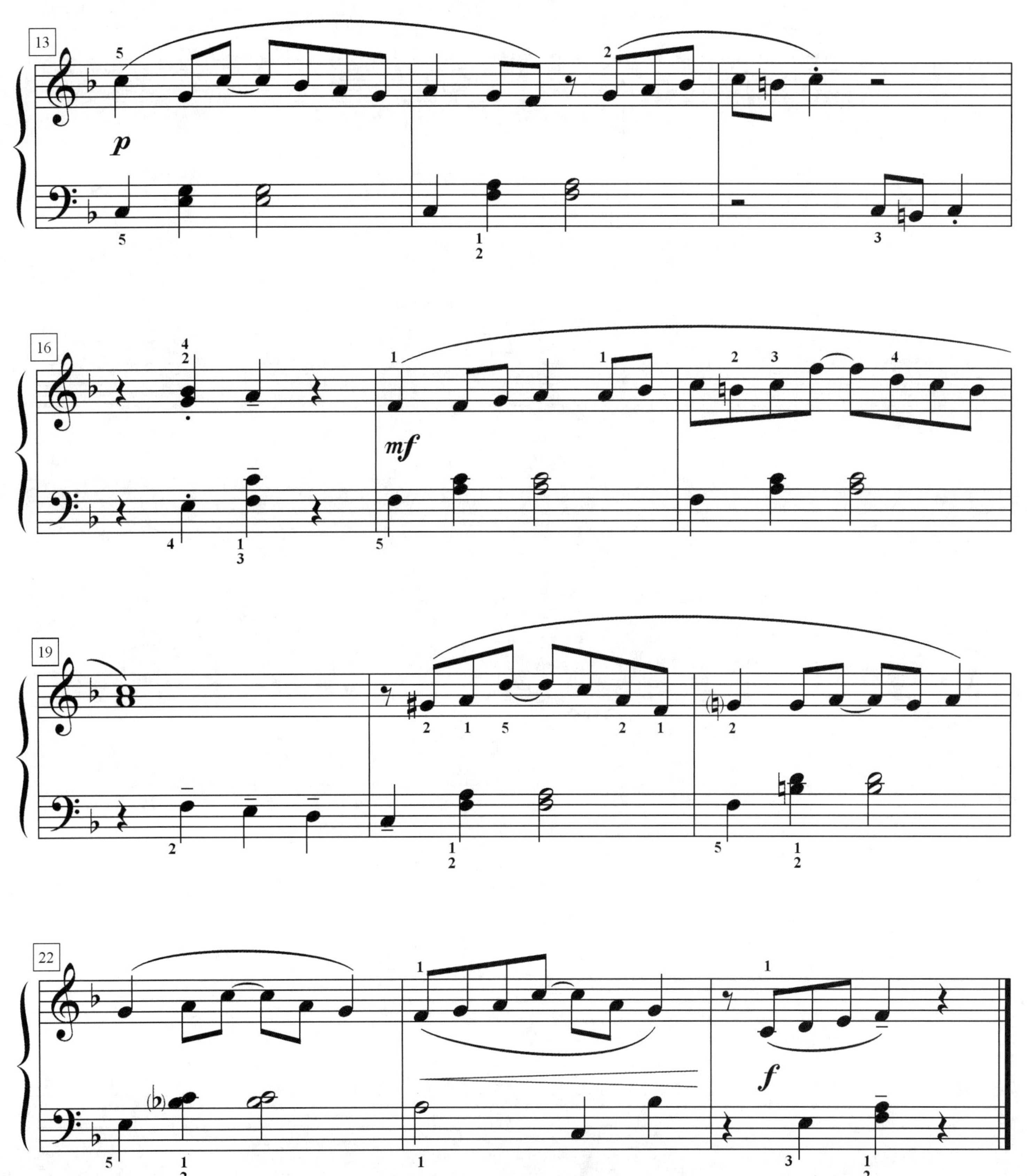

13
p
16
mf
19
22
f

Maple Leaf Rag

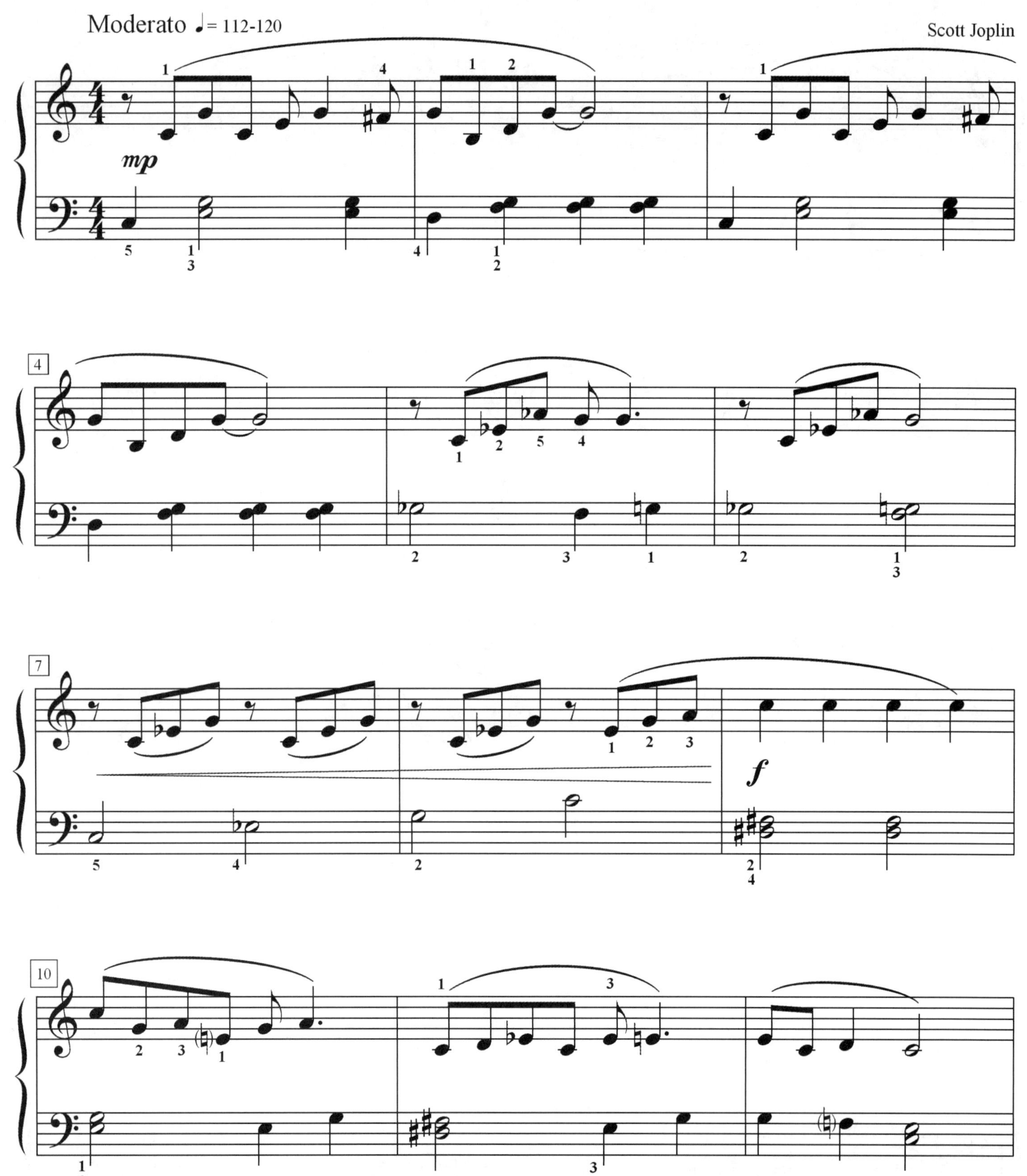

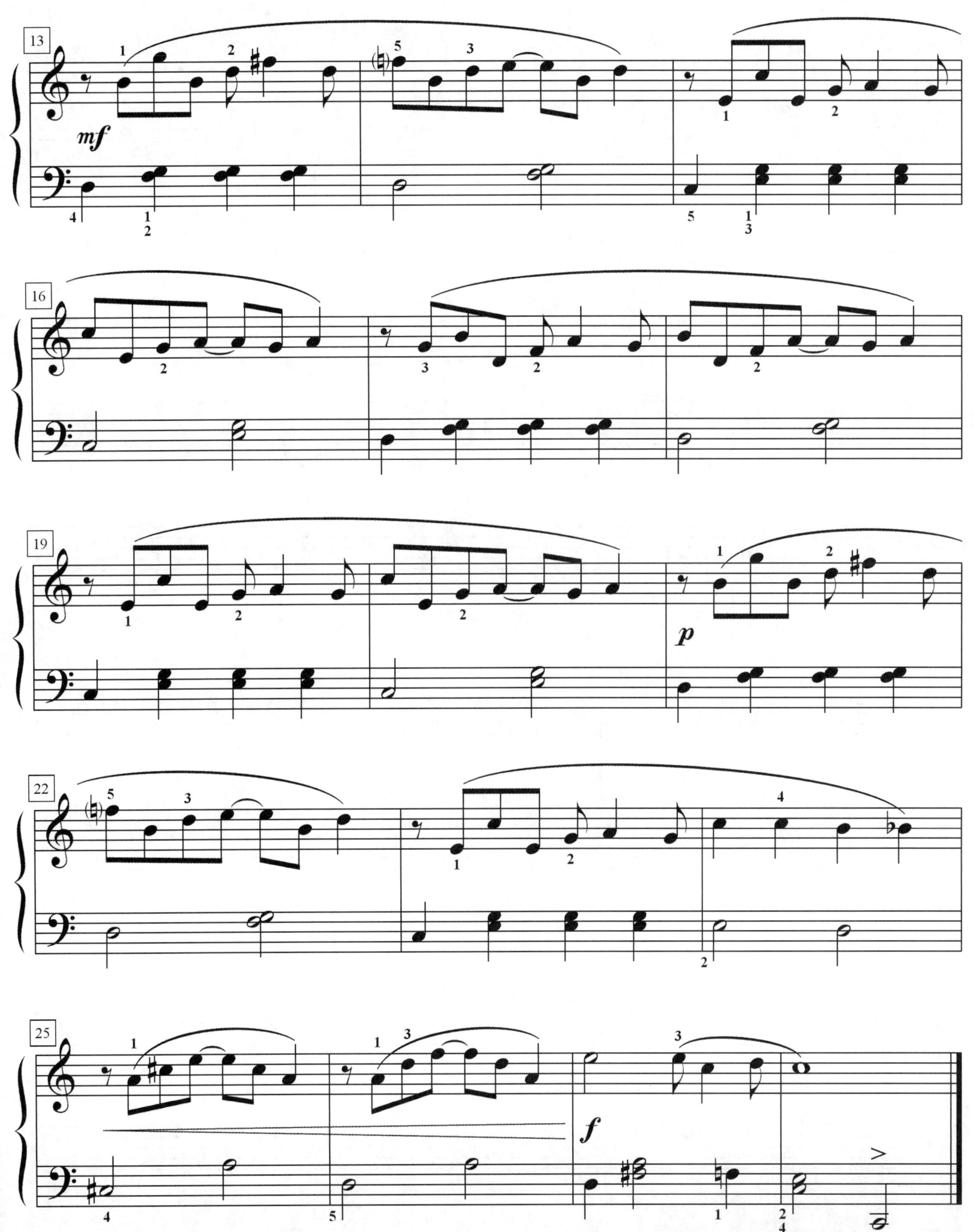

13
mf
16
19
p
22
25
f

Big City Rag

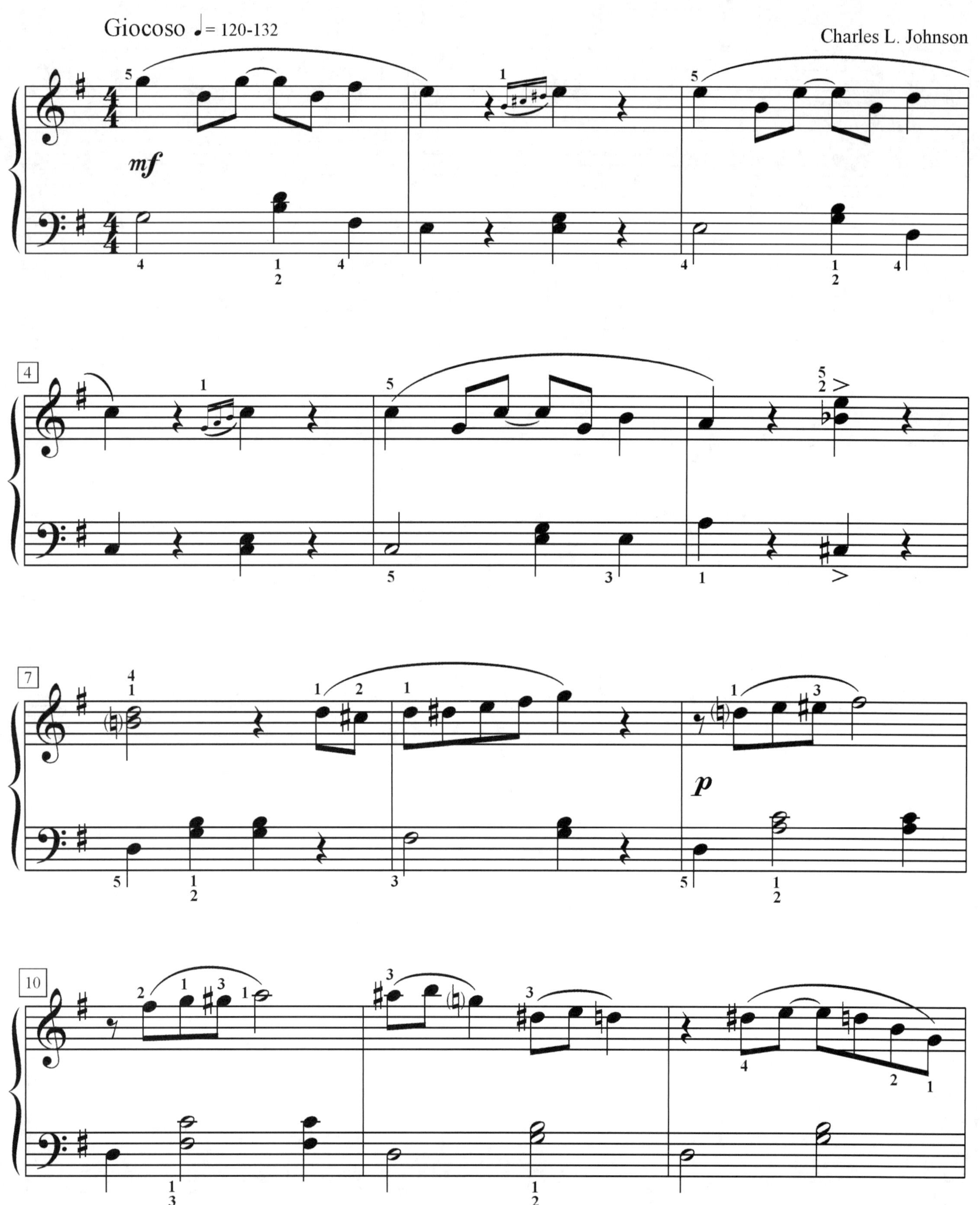

Giocoso ♩ = 120-132
Charles L. Johnson
mf
p